From A to Z

From A to Z

Manipulatives in Reading

Lilia Burton
Author

Illustrated by: Lilia Burton and
Kim Mahal Laude

Library of Congress Control Number: 2006909278
ISBN: Hardcover   978-1-4257-3905-8
               Softcover   978-1-4257-3904-1

To order additional copies of this book, contact:
Xlibris Corporation
1-888-795-4274
www.Xlibris.com
Orders@Xlibris.com
37239

Contents

Dedication

To my grandmother, Deonesia Bautista, who went to heaven without knowing how to read or write, my aunt Salustiana Bautista who believed in me and helped me believe that I have the power to help others, my father Tranquilino Opina who supported many of my ambitions and encouraged me to become somebody who will make a difference in the lives of many children, my mother Francisca Bautista Opina, who was my first teacher who taught me to be patient, creative, compassionate, and committed to bringing success to everyone.

Book Description

This book is a collection of manipulative materials from A to Z. The purpose of this book is to provide activities that make sense to diverse learners and learning experiences that are fun for beginning or struggling readers. The activities in this book focus on phonological awareness skills, letters/sound recognition and writing, as well as spelling practice, and reading sight words. In addition, a collection of selected nouns is included to enhance vocabulary and comprehension, including synonyms, antonyms, homophone, and compound words. I personally developed over the years the activities included in this book to help teachers and parents enhance the children's learning process. The activities in this book assist parents in helping their children at home to improve oral reading fluency. Furthermore, the drawings in this book allow the children to understand each word through picture recognition. Lastly, this book is a result of my 12 years of teaching experience and knowledge of improving academic achievement.

This book is a good learning resource to have in the classroom, to support cooperative learning concept for small group instruction, partner learning, and individual or independent learning at the centers. In addition, parents can benefit from this book by working with their own children at home. Children can also have centers at home to enjoy their moments and have fun learning together, with their parents, siblings, and relatives.

Finally, this book is relevant and useful in any place for all types of learners. I am confident that this book will be an effective reading resource for beginning and struggling readers.

The objectives in this book align with the Alabama Course of Study: English Language Arts, Bulletin (1999).

- Recognizing and naming upper- and lower-case letters.
- Recognizing sound-print relationships.
- Identifying the vowels and consonant sounds.
- Understanding the letter-sound correspondence.

- Understanding picture-word association.
- Counting sounds in words.
- Manipulating the sounds of the English language.
- Creating patterns in language to create meaning.
- Blending sounds to form words.
- Spelling words correctly.
- Connecting text, message heard, or material viewed to prior knowledge and experiences.
- Writing legible formation of letters and appropriate spacing.
- Reading accurately, quickly, with expression and comprehension
- Expanding vocabulary and sentence awareness.
- Applying principles of grammar in written expression.

The contents in this book will be used in my study of effective intervention of struggling readers. This book's focus skills are:

- Listening
- Writing
- Viewing
- Speaking
- Spelling

- Reading
- Fluency
- Vocabulary
- Comprehension
- Critical thinking

- Self-expression
- Creative art
- Phonics
- Phonemic awareness
- Decoding

Preface

My purpose in developing manipulatives is to present an effective intervention for struggling readers in kindergarten through grade 3. According to Woods (2002) and Work (2002), the term manipulatives involve objects that can be moved by hands or operated manually to enhance learning. Manipulatives are objects that involve the use of hands, muscles and eyes that help children develop coordination and problem solving skills (Work, 2002). In my 12 years as a teacher, mentor, tutor, as well as a learner, I have worked in different schools in two different states. My observations during my years in education including the years when my children were in primary grades has been the needs of students, parents, and teachers in the area of beginning reading instruction. My experiences as a teacher lead me to believe that students are thrown in with ineffective intervention of struggling readers. I found that only the established readers are capable of learning from the basal reader during the whole group instruction. Established readers are students who read a text accurately and quickly with expression as well as focusing their attention on the meaning of the text. With limited funding for resources and professional staff, teachers are not getting the support for the training and materials necessary to teach reading in early childhood. The students suffer and many are left struggling to learn to read. These students become struggling readers. Struggling readers are students who are having difficulty in learning to read successfully because their attention and time is spent mostly on "figuring out the words, leaving them little attention for understanding the text (Armbruster, Lehr & Osborne, 2001, p. 22). In addition struggling readers are also identified as "at-risk" students because they are at risk of reading failures. Speece and Ritchey (2005) defined "at risk" as students with academic performance "in the bottom of 25th percentile of their class" (p.389).

Effective reading intervention consists of phonological awareness that includes phonemic awareness. Armbruster, Lehr, and Osborn (2001) describe phonemic awareness as the "ability to hear, identify, and manipulate the individual sounds-phonemes in spoken words. In addition to phonemes, phonological awareness activities can involve work with rhymes, words, syllables, and onset and rimes (p. 4). The use of teacher created manipulatives was developed to support the activities involved in phonological awareness. Providing reading intervention to more than a half of students usually 12 to 14 students out of 22 or more in a whole class is increasingly difficult to accomplish success. In my experience, I found it easier to divide the 12 to 14 struggling students into two smaller groups of six to seven, each group using manipulatives through cooperative learning or partner reading while intervention is delivered daily on a one-on-one basis or while reading assessment is being conducted. One-on-one instruction provides effective intervention of struggling readers however manipulatives and hands-on activities must be included to provide a quality instruction that makes sense for a struggling reader as well as for all children in order to achieve maximum growth.

Since I started teaching and in the past 12 years, my focus and attention have been on the development of manipulatives and phonological awareness that would provide effective intervention of struggling readers from kindergarten through grade 3 as well as effective center activities for all students. My primary concern in developing the activities included in this book is simple enough to follow by students, teachers, and parents. In addition, this book is usable in a classroom setting, at home, or independent learning anywhere. I have reviewed several literatures regarding struggling readers and knowing the areas of concerns surrounding this subject, I extend my greatest respect to the researchers and their research done. Although my research is just beginning, I am confident that the activities included in this book will provide best practices in the early intervention of struggling readers from kindergarten through grade 3.

I know that this book can be used as a reading resource for parents and teachers as well as in reading intervention programs with individuals or small groups of beginning or struggling readers. Lastly, this book aims to help every child become an established reader.

Foreword

Love, life, and learning describe Mrs. Lilia Burton. In 1995, she played many roles as a member of the Chicago, Illinois, Field School staff such as implementing the teaching techniques of "learning styles". Mrs. Burton also achieved great parent involvement in her classroom and within the school to improve students' achievement.

Mrs. Lilia Burton is definitely an extremely professional individual who is reliable and dependable. She takes a great deal of initiative and pride in her work as a teacher, artist, and a writer. She is always motivated to do her best. Her positive attitude makes her presence at work even more valuable to anyone she has contact with.

As a teacher/mentor, tutor, workshop presenter, and a team member, Mrs. Burton is patient, kind, and compassionate. She has taught second grade students with diverse personalities and ethnic backgrounds both in bilingual and monolingual classrooms. Students, parents, and community members have found her to be accessible, friendly, and professional. Her colleagues find her leadership skills and professional expertise very helpful in improving their personal and professional lives.

Mrs. Lilia Burton does an excellent job in whatever roles she is ask to fill. She is responsible and conscientious while also displaying her creative talents in ways to enhance the experience of the learners in school and outside the school environment.

Jude Laude and Kimberly Laude
President and Director of
Kuumba Before and After School Youth Program
17013 South Magnolia Drive
Hazel Crest, Illinois 60429

Acknowledgement

During the years 1995-1997, the strength of a family was tested by ambition and a desire for a change. Change is good because it improves the quality of life however it takes love and commitment to make it work. It is my greatest pleasure and pride with sincere affection that James Burton Jr., the man I have known since 1973 is the man who had all the strength to carry me through the many changes in my life. He took care of our family and never complained while I completed my Masters of Education degree. Being an educator, I believe that learning should not stop therefore I am again pursuing a higher degree in education. In the year 2005 and currently, I am completing my doctoral degree in education and James Burton Jr. was again tested by my desire to better myself personally and professionally. This too is a change and he is still standing behind me with full strength and trust that this too will soon be over successfully.

I realized that some of the most difficult task was made possible by my wonderful daughter Jennifer. Her unending assistance and willingness to help however long the time demands is moving. I give Jennifer my special thanks for being there at all times. My sincere thanks go to Kimberly Laude, who is the older of my two daughters, for listening to me during the times that she, herself needed someone to listen. Her inspiring drawings show that she put her heart through her talent to support me in everything and anything under the sun. To my grandchildren Solomon, Najidah, Kwisi, and Azubuike who contributed their ideas on what to include in my book, I give them the biggest hugs in the world.

Last and foremost, I cannot forget the support from my colleagues especially Miss Steele, Mrs. Oliviere, Mr. Wood and Dr. Walker. Their hard work and dedication for the success of all children was my inspiration to continue the many things that I want to experience. Many thanks to the parents who participated in the make and take workshop and allowed their children to have fun in learning with manipulatives. My special thanks go to the many children who took interest in the hands-on learning activities at home or in school and learned from the contents of this book. It is with my greatest pleasure to see their faces as they find success in learning to read with comfort. As I see a difference in each child's life, I see a bright future for all children making our world a better place to live.

Research Study

Broad research topic: Manipulative Tools and Phonological Awareness: Intervention of Struggling Readers

The general area being examined in this research topic is the learning needs of struggling readers. The theory of learning from Blanchard's (2000) research suggests "using phonological awareness as an early intervention in primary grades would prevent reading failures" (p. 20). Therefore, the focus of this broad topic is to improve the reading fluency of struggling readers by providing them with reading intervention and practice skills in phonological and phonemic awareness. However, in addition to a small group and one-on-one reading intervention in a classroom setting, struggling readers also need support from tutors, volunteer readers and their family members to provide reading skills that focus on elements such as the letters and sounds of the alphabet.

Leafstedt, Richards, and Gerber (2004) defined phonological awareness as an understanding of the sound structure of oral language in the early reading development. The authors suggested that children have difficulties in "reading fluently and comprehension of written text when they have difficulty understanding that words can be broken into individual phonemes" (p.251). Norman and Calfee (2004) suggested that once phonemic awareness skills were acquired, such as producing letter sounds in their mouths, children can move quickly toward becoming independent readers.

Narrow research topic: The Effectiveness of Phonological Awareness Manipulatives in the Reading Intervention of Second-grade Struggling Readers

The specific area of this research being examined is the effectiveness of phonological awareness manipulatives in the reading intervention of second-grade struggling readers. In a constructivist theory of learning, phonological awareness is blended into manipulative tools to enhance the reading fluency of struggling readers. Dewey (2005) argued "that education is not an affair of telling and being told, but an active and constructive process" (p. 46). He further argued that bringing connections to consciousness enhances the meaning of the experience. Therefore, the manipulatives would provide the connections to acquiring fluency in a way that makes sense for a struggling reader.

Problem statement:

The problem is when children do not get early reading intervention; they have difficulty in learning to read. Steiner (1997) argued that "if you had some prior knowledge of a subject, you can easily relearn when you need it again" (p.212). Therefore, providing children with reading practice and skills in naming and sounding the letters of the alphabet is important because it prevents reading failures. The lack of reading practice or prior knowledge of letters and sounds of the alphabet is not the only reason why a child might struggle to read. When children's "learning styles mismatch their previous reading instruction, they have not learned to read" according to Carbo, Dunn and Dunn (1991, p. 31). In contrast, the problem according to D'Arcangelo's (2003) interview with Dr. Sally Shaywitz is that "children with reading problems had phonologic difficulties" (p. 5). Therefore, teaching phonemic awareness and letter-sound relationships enhance reading fluency and a child's ability to learn to read. However, only few researches were done regarding the use of phonological awareness manipulatives in the reading intervention of primary grades.

Purpose of study:

The purpose of this study is to help K-3 struggling readers acquire skills in phonological and phonemic awareness using manipulatives in reading intervention. In order to provide an appropriate reading intervention to enhance the reading fluency of struggling readers, teacher created manipulatives will be used at the learning centers to provide struggling readers with opportunities to work with other children with different levels of learning. The manipulatives involve hands-on activities that will fully engage children in small group learning, partner learning, or independent learning. In addition, manipulatives will be used by parents at home to help their children acquire skills needed in reading fluency.

Research questions:

Based on the study's purpose, the following questions will be addressed on an on-going basis.

- "How do teachers identify children who have difficulty in reading?"
- "What kinds of manipulatives are appropriate for the intervention of struggling readers?"
- "When do we need to use the manipulative materials and how long? Why?"

Theoretical or Conceptual Framework:

The research topic is based on two theoretical frameworks. The first theoretical framework is the cultural-historical theory of learning by Vygotsky. Vygotsky (1986) argued that the use of objects lead children toward cognitive mastery. Vygotsky's concept of psychological and material tools serves as "mediator between the human hand and the object upon which the tool acts" (p. xxiv). The cultural-historical theory of learning by Vygotsky was used by Bodrova and Leong (2001) to study the Vygotskian approach in American early childhood and primary classrooms. The authors argued that "the process of learning cultural tools begins in the early years when children first encounter artifacts and procedures associated with using them; they learn to use language to communicate with other people and later regulate their own behavior" (p. 12). Bodrova and Leong further argued that arming children with necessary tools and learning from them repeatedly over and over in fun and engaging activities will help children to remember things. The authors suggested that Vygotsky's theory of learning and his concept of psychological and material process of learning and development will lead to higher mental functions. The second theoretical framework in this study is the constructivist theory of learning by John Dewey. Lambert, Walker, Zimmerman, Cooper, Lambert, et. al. (2002) suggested that Dewey's foundation of constructivist theory of learning notes that students must learn and make sense of new knowledge by connecting to their prior knowledge. In addition, the authors suggested that Dewey's perception of learning as a social construction of knowledge is based on his concept of cooperative learning. Furthermore, Lambert et. al. suggested that Dewey set the stage for the emergence of constructivist thought and Jean

Piaget expanded our understanding of learning in ways that support and contribute to constructivism. Dewey's constructivist theory of learning was used by Norman and Calfee's (2004) study on a hands-on approach for assessing phonics. The authors used manipulative materials such as the test tiles for assessing students' skill in phonics. Additionally, the author's study supported the use of manipulative materials as means of acquiring phonological awareness skill in a way that makes sense. As applied to this study, the independent variables (factors) that will or will not affect outcome will be the use of manipulative materials in the instruction of phonological awareness and the treatment of struggling readers. Based on Vygotsky's theory as well as the cognitive theory of learning, this study will be applied to a group of 10 African-American boys and girls who will be selected from a second-grade classroom. The boys and girls who will participate in this study will be divided into two groups. Group A (Experimental Group) will be treated with the use of manipulative materials as well as reading decodable books. These manipulative materials will be used in centers, small group instruction, paired learning, individual learning, or one-on one tutoring to determine the effectiveness in the intervention of second-grade struggling readers. Group B (Control Group) will not be treated with manipulative materials however they will read decodable books and use supplemental materials such as worksheets to improve their reading fluency. Group A and Group B's reading scores will be evaluated in the middle of school year. The basis of comparison will be the participants' ability to read accurately and quickly. The dependent variable (result) or expected outcome in this study will indicate that Group A (Experimental Group) will improve on a higher scale than Group B (Control Group) in oral reading fluency. Finally in this study, the expected result will support the concept of blending manipulatives and phonological awareness skills in the intervention of second-grade struggling readers.

Definition of Terms:

Defining all five terms in this study is important because it will help parents and teachers in identifying the area of a child's difficulty in reading. In the research of Armbruster, Lehr, and Osborn (2002), the following concepts were introduced to teachers and found to have a positive impact on the children's reading scores when used appropriately. The terms that will be used frequently in this study are as follow:

- fluency—is the ability to read text accurately and quickly with expression and comprehension.
- phonemic awareness—is the ability to notice, think about, and work with individual sounds in spoken words.
- phonological awareness—is a recognition of how sounds can be manipulated and how they are parts of spoken language.

Woods (2002) used the term manipulative materials in his study to define alphabet that can be moved by hands. Work (2002) used the term manipulatives center to define the area where small groups can play games, construct, fit things together or develop patterns. Additionally according to Woods and Work's definitions, the term manipulatives involve objects that can be moved by hands or operated manually to enhance learning. The terms below are the most important definitions to remember in this study.

- manipulatives—are objects that involve the use of hands, muscles and eyes that help children develop coordination and problem solving skills (Work, 2002).
- struggling reader—is a student who reads at a level of frustration, a level at which this student cannot comfortably succeed (Tyner, 2004).

Scope and Delimitations:

Initially, this study will search for knowledge or information about the characteristics of a struggling reader. The information will be gathered through literature reviews, personal interviews, question and answer notations during teacher in-service discussions, and written evaluations of workshop presentations. The compiled information will help teachers to identify children who have difficulty in reading. By identifying the children who will have difficulty in learning to read, teachers will be able to design appropriate intervention to prevent struggling readers from reading failures (Blanchard, 2000). Manipulative materials that support phonological and phonemic awareness will be used to provide hands-on learning experience in fun and meaningful ways. A limitation of this study involves the lack of research in the areas of reading manipulatives and the intervention of second-grade struggling readers. More research on hands-on learning and manipulatives is needed to support a successful intervention of struggling readers.

Significance of the Study:

The significance of the study will impact on the students' academic achievement. The phonological awareness and manipulative materials will provide practice skills to improve students' fluency according to the national standards. This study will inspire teachers, parents, students, and others who are involved in children's education to use manipulatives that promote phonological awareness skills. Children who are learning to read English as their second language (ESL) as well as children with reading disabilities will experience hands-on learning activities in a way that makes sense. To support the significance of this study, this experimenter read other research including Leafstedt, Richards, and Gerber's (2004) study examining the effects of phonological awareness instruction for kindergarten English learners. The authors surveyed seventeen English learner students who spoke Spanish at home and one student who was exposed to Spanish through extended family and spoke only English at home. Leafstedt, Richards, and Gerber's research suggested that when students lack phonological awareness, they are greatly disadvantaged in learning how to decode new words. In addition, the authors suggested that "problems with decoding lead to further difficulties in reading fluently and comprehension of written test" (p. 252). Leafstedt, Richards, and Gerber concluded that phonological awareness is an acquired skill that is available to students regardless of which language they speak. In another research similar to Leafstedt, Richards, and Gerber's study, Smith (2003) indicated that "students who entered primary grades without phonemic awareness might have reading difficulties" (p. 3). Finally, this study will bring significance to children who read according to their learning style. Carbo, Dunn and Dunn (1991) suggested that children will learn to read effectively when their reading instruction matches their learning styles.

Submitted to: Walden University (7/2006)
EDUC 8015: Research Approaches for the Teacher Leader

Pronunciation Sounds

Lilia Burton (9/1995)

- Read the underlined letter/s then say the sound/s.
- Spell the words then sound it out.
- If the word has two or more syllables, break it down into parts. Read the parts.
- Blend the parts smoothly while sounding out the word.
- Read the word again, at least three times or when reading is accurate and automatic.

a ...... m**a**p, n**a**p, t**a**p, p**a**tch

a ...... d**ay**, tod**ay**, d**a**te, f**a**te

a ...... f**a**ther, **au**nt, h**au**nt, **aw**e

e ...... b**e**d, r**e**d, s**e**t, w**e**t

ea .... **ea**sy, **ea**t, b**ea**t, h**ea**t

ee .... b**ee**t, b**ee**tle, f**ee**t, t**ee**th

i .... s**i**p, sk**i**p, t**i**p, tr**i**p

i .... b**i**te, k**i**te, s**i**te, t**i**de

igh ... h**igh**, r**igh**t, s**igh**, t**igh**t

o ...... b**o**ne, st**o**ne, t**o**ne, z**o**ne

o ...... b**o**ther, br**o**ther, c**o**t, r**o**t

oo .... b**oo**k, c**oo**k, t**oo**k, f**oo**t

oi ..... b**oi**l, c**oi**l, s**oi**l, sp**oi**l

ow ... bl**ow**, fl**ow**, l**ow**, sn**ow**

ow ... b**ow**, c**ow**, pl**ow**, w**ow**

oy .... b**oy**, j**oy**, s**oy**, t**oy**

u ...... r**u**n, s**u**n, **u**nder, **u**mbrella

u ...... c**u**re, p**u**re, c**u**te, m**u**te

u ...... b**u**sh, p**u**sh, p**u**ll, p**u**t

ch .... ba**tch**, ca**tch**, **ch**in, **ch**ur**ch**

sh ..... hu**sh**, mu**sh**, **sh**ine, **sh**y

th ..... **th**en, **th**in, **th**ing, **th**ink

wh ... **wh**ale, **wh**en, **wh**ich, **wh**ite

ang.. b**ang**, f**ang**, g**ang**, s**ang**

ing ... br**ing**, k**ing**, r**ing**, s**ing**

ong.. bel**ong**, l**ong**, s**ong**, str**ong**

ung.. h**ung**, l**ung**, r**ung**, s**ung**

b ...... **b**a**b**y, **b**i**b**, cri**b**, ri**b**

c ...... **c**law, **c**lean, **c**ling, **c**lo**ck**

d ...... a**dd**, **d**a**d**, **d**i**d**, fi**dd**le

f .... cu**ff**, **fi**fty, **fl**u**ff**y, o**ff**

g ...... bi**g**, fi**g**, **g**et, **g**o

h ...... **h**ang, **h**at, **h**eat, **h**unt

j........ **j**ack, **j**acket, **j**et, **j**ob

k ...... **k**ic**k**, **k**ind, **k**it, **k**itchen

l........ coo**l**, **l**i**l**y, **l**ong, pa**l**e

m ..... di**m**, **m**an, **m**oon, **m**ur**m**ur

n ...... **n**i**n**e, **n**oo**n**, **n**o**n**e, ow**n**

p ...... li**p**, **p**e**pp**er, **p**i**p**e, **p**o**p**

q ...... **q**uail, **q**uarter, **q**ueen, **q**uit

r .... **r**a**r**e, **r**ate, **r**oa**r**, **r**ust

s .... le**ss**, **s**et, **s**i**s**ter, **s**nake

t .... a**tt**ach, a**tt**ack, **t**igh**t**, **t**o**t**e

v ...... gi**v**e, **v**isa, vi**v**a, **v**i**v**id

w...... a**w**ay, **w**ay, **w**e, **w**o**w**

x ...... a**x**e, a**x**is, o**x**, **x**-ray

y ...... **y**ard, **y**ear, **y**east, **y**oke

z....... ja**zz**, **z**ebra, **z**ero, **z**ig**z**ag

Pronunciation Sound Cards

Lilia Burton (Redesigned 9/2005)

The pronunciation cards on pages 5 through 12 have been arranged so that it will correspond with the sound/words on pages 13 through 20. The purpose of this arrangement is for double-side copying.

References:
The New Merriam-Webster Dictionary (1981). Merriam-Webster Inc.
Merriam-Webster's Elementary Dictionary (1994). Merriam-Webster Inc.
Educational Insights, Inc. (2000) Rancho Dominguez, CA

Pronunciation Sound(1995, 2005)
Card 2

a

LOB Educational Services   Liliaburton@aol.com

Pronunciation Sound(1995, 2005)
Card 1

a

LOB Educational Services   Liliaburton@aol.com

Pronunciation Sound(1995, 2005)
Card 4

e

LOB Educational Services   Liliaburton@aol.com

Pronunciation Sound(1995, 2005)
Card 3

a

LOB Educational Services   Liliaburton@aol.com

Pronunciation Sound(1995, 2005)
Card 6

ee

LOB Educational Services   Liliaburton@aol.com

Pronunciation Sound(1995, 2005)
Card 5

ea

LOB Educational Services   Liliaburton@aol.com

Pronunciation Sounds

a as in . . . .

m**a**p   n**a**p
p**a**tch   t**a**p

LOB Educational Services   Liliaburton@aol.com

Pronunciation Sounds

a as in . . . .

d**ay**   tod**ay**
d**a**te   f**a**te

LOB Educational Services   Liliaburton@aol.com

Pronunciation Sounds

a as in . . . .

f**a**ther   **au**nt
h**au**nt   **aw**e

LOB Educational Services   Liliaburton@aol.com

Pronunciation Sounds

e as in . . . .

b**e**d   r**e**d
s**e**t   w**e**t

LOB Educational Services   Liliaburton@aol.com

Pronunciation Sounds

ea as in . . . .

easy   **ea**t
b**ea**t   h**ea**t

LOB Educational Services   Liliaburton@aol.com

Pronunciation Sounds

ee as in . . . .

b**ee**t   t**ee**th
f**ee**t   b**ee**tle

LOB Educational Services   Liliaburton@aol.com

Pronunciation Sound(1995, 2005)
Card 8

i

LOB Educational Services   Liliaburton@aol.com

Pronunciation Sound(1995, 2005)
Card 7

i

LOB Educational Services   Liliaburton@aol.com

Pronunciation Sound(1995, 2005)
Card 10

LOB Educational Services   Liliaburton@aol.com

Pronunciation Sound(1995, 2005)
Card 9

LOB Educational Services   Liliaburton@aol.com

Pronunciation Sound(1995, 2005)
Card 12

LOB Educational Services   Liliaburton@aol.com

Pronunciation Sound(1995, 2005)
Card 11

LOB Educational Services   Liliaburton@aol.com

Pronunciation Sounds

i as in . . . .

s**i**p   sk**i**p
t**i**p   tr**i**p

Pronunciation Sounds

i as in . . . .

b**i**te   k**i**te
s**i**te   t**i**de

Pronunciation Sounds

igh as in . . . .

h**igh**   r**igh**t
s**igh**   t**igh**t

Pronunciation Sounds

o as in . . . .

b**o**ne   st**o**ne
t**o**ne   z**o**ne

Pronunciation Sounds

o as in . . . .

b**o**ther   c**o**t
br**o**ther   r**o**t

Pronunciation Sounds

oo as in . . . .

b**oo**k   c**oo**k
t**oo**k   f**oo**t

Pronunciation Sound(1995, 2005) Card 14 **ow** LOB Educational Services Liliaburton@aol.com	Pronunciation Sound(1995, 2005) Card 13 **oi** LOB Educational Services Liliaburton@aol.com
Pronunciation Sound(1995, 2005) Card 16 **oy** LOB Educational Services Liliaburton@aol.com	Pronunciation Sound(1995, 2005) Card 15 **ow**  LOB Educational Services Liliaburton@aol.com
Pronunciation Sound(1995, 2005) Card 18 **U** LOB Educational Services Liliaburton@aol.com	Pronunciation Sound(1995, 2005) Card 17 **U** LOB Educational Services Liliaburton@aol.com

Pronunciation Sounds

oi as in . . . .

b**oi**l   c**oi**l
s**oi**l   sp**oi**l

Pronunciation Sounds

ow as in . . . .

bl**ow**   fl**ow**
l**ow**   sn**ow**

Pronunciation Sounds

ow as in . . . .

b**ow**   c**ow**
pl**ow**   w**ow**

Pronunciation Sounds

oy as in . . . .

b**oy**   j**oy**
s**oy**   t**oy**

Pronunciation Sounds

U as in . . . .

r**u**n   s**u**n
under
umbrella

Pronunciation Sounds

U as in . . . .

c**u**re   p**u**re
c**u**te   m**u**te

Pronunciation Sound(1995, 2005)
Card 20

ch

LOB Educational Services   Liliaburton@aol.com

Pronunciation Sound(1995, 2005)
Card 19

u

LOB Educational Services   Liliaburton@aol.com

Pronunciation Sound(1995, 2005)
Card 22

th

LOB Educational Services   Liliaburton@aol.com

Pronunciation Sound(1995, 2005)
Card 21

sh

LOB Educational Services   Liliaburton@aol.com

Pronunciation Sound(1995, 2005)
Card 24

ang

LOB Educational Services   Liliaburton@aol.com

Pronunciation Sound(1995, 2005)
Card 23

wh

LOB Educational Services   Liliaburton@aol.com

Pronunciation Sounds

U as in . . . .

b**u**sh   p**u**sh
p**u**ll   p**u**t

Pronunciation Sounds

ch as in . . . .

bat**ch**   **ch**in
cat**ch**
chur**ch**

Pronunciation Sounds

sh as in . . . .

hu**sh**   mu**sh**
shine   **sh**y

Pronunciation Sounds

th as in . . . .

then   **th**in
thing   **th**ink

Pronunciation Sounds

wh as in . . . .

whale
when
which **wh**ite

Pronunciation Sounds

ang as in . . . .

b**ang**   f**ang**
g**ang**   s**ang**

Pronunciation Sound(1995, 2005)
Card 26

ong

LOB Educational Services   Liliaburton@aol.com

Pronunciation Sound(1995, 2005)
Card 25

ing

LOB Educational Services   Liliaburton@aol.com

Pronunciation Sound(1995, 2005)
Card 28

b

LOB Educational Services   Liliaburton@aol.com

Pronunciation Sound(1995, 2005)
Card 27

ung

LOB Educational Services   Liliaburton@aol.com

Pronunciation Sound(1995, 2005)
Card 30

d

LOB Educational Services   Liliaburton@aol.com

Pronunciation Sound(1995, 2005)
Card 29

c

LOB Educational Services   Liliaburton@aol.com

Pronunciation Sounds

ing as in . . . .

br**ing** k**ing**
r**ing** s**ing**

Pronunciation Sounds

ong as in . . . .

bel**ong** l**ong**
s**ong** str**ong**

Pronunciation Sounds

ung as in . . . .

h**ung** l**ung**
r**ung** s**ung**

Pronunciation Sounds

b as in . . . .

ba**b**y **b**i**b**
cri**b** ri**b**

Pronunciation Sounds

c as in . . . .

claw **c**lean
cling **c**lock

Pronunciation Sounds

d as in . . . .

a**dd** **d**a**d**
di**d** fi**dd**le

Pronunciation Sound(1995, 2005)
Card 32

g

LOB Educational Services   Liliaburton@aol.com

Pronunciation Sound(1995, 2005)
Card 31

f

LOB Educational Services   Liliaburton@aol.com

Pronunciation Sound(1995, 2005)
Card 34

j

LOB Educational Services   Liliaburton@aol.com

Pronunciation Sound(1995, 2005)
Card 33

LOB Educational Services   Liliaburton@aol.com

Pronunciation Sound(1995, 2005)
Card 36

LOB Educational Services   Liliaburton@aol.com

Pronunciation Sound(1995, 2005)
Card 35

LOB Educational Services   Liliaburton@aol.com

Pronunciation Sounds

f as in . . . .

cu**ff**   **fif**ty

flu**ff**y   o**ff**

LOB Educational Services   Liliaburton@aol.com

Pronunciation Sounds

g as in . . . .

bi**g**   fi**g**

get   **g**o

LOB Educational Services   Liliaburton@aol.com

Pronunciation Sounds

h as in . . . .

hang   **h**at

heat   **h**unt

LOB Educational Services   Liliaburton@aol.com

Pronunciation Sounds

j as in . . . .

jack   **j**acket

jet   **j**ob

LOB Educational Services   Liliaburton@aol.com

Pronunciation Sounds

k as in . . . .

kic**k**   **k**ind

kit   **k**itchen

LOB Educational Services   Liliaburton@aol.com

Pronunciation Sounds

l as in . . . .

coo**l**   **l**i**l**y

long   pa**l**e

LOB Educational Services   Liliaburton@aol.com

Pronunciation Sound(1995, 2005)
Card 44

n

LOB Educational Services   Liliaburton@aol.com

Pronunciation Sound(1995, 2005)
Card 43

LOB Educational Services   Liliaburton@aol.com

Pronunciation Sound(1995, 2005)
Card 46

q

LOB Educational Services   Liliaburton@aol.com

Pronunciation Sound(1995, 2005)
Card 45

LOB Educational Services   Liliaburton@aol.com

Pronunciation Sound(1995, 2005)
Card 48

s

LOB Educational Services   Liliaburton@aol.com

Pronunciation Sound(1995, 2005)
Card 47

LOB Educational Services   Liliaburton@aol.com

Pronunciation Sounds

m as in . . . .
di**m**
man **m**oon
mur**m**ur

Pronunciation Sounds

n as in . . . .
ni**n**e   **n**oo**n**
no**n**e   ow**n**

LOB Educational Services   Liliaburton@aol.com

Pronunciation Sounds

p as in . . . .
li**p**   **p**e**pp**er
pi**p**e   **p**o**p**

LOB Educational Services   Liliaburton@aol.com

Pronunciation Sounds

q as in . . . .
quail   **q**uit
quarter
queen

Pronunciation Sounds

r as in . . . .
ra**r**e   **r**ate
roa**r**   **r**ust

LOB Educational Services   Liliaburton@aol.com

Pronunciation Sounds

s as in . . . .
le**ss**   **s**et
si**s**ter **s**nake

LOB Educational Services   Liliaburton@aol.com

Pronunciation Sound(1995, 2005)
Card 44

LOB Educational Services   Liliaburton@aol.com

Pronunciation Sound(1995, 2005)
Card 43

LOB Educational Services   Liliaburton@aol.com

Pronunciation Sound(1995, 2005)
Card 46

LOB Educational Services   Liliaburton@aol.com

Pronunciation Sound(1995, 2005)
Card 45

LOB Educational Services   Liliaburton@aol.com

Pronunciation Sound(1995, 2005)
Card 48

LOB Educational Services   Liliaburton@aol.com

Pronunciation Sound(1995, 2005)
Card 47

LOB Educational Services   Liliaburton@aol.com

Pronunciation Sounds

t as in . . . .

a**tt**ach **t**igh**t**
a**tt**ack **t**o**t**e

LOB Educational Services   Liliaburton@aol.com

Pronunciation Sounds

v as in . . . .

gi**v**e **v**isa
vi**v**a **viv**id

LOB Educational Services   Liliaburton@aol.com

Pronunciation Sounds

w as in . . . .

a**w**ay **w**ay
we **w**o**w**

LOB Educational Services   Liliaburton@aol.com

Pronunciation Sounds

x as in . . . .

a**x**e a**x**is
o**x** **x**-ray

LOB Educational Services   Liliaburton@aol.com

Pronunciation Sounds

y as in . . . .

yard **y**ear
yeast **y**oke

LOB Educational Services   Liliaburton@aol.com

Pronunciation Sounds

z as in . . . .

ja**zz** **z**ebra
zero **z**ig**z**ag

LOB Educational Services   Liliaburton@aol.com

Lower Case Alphabet (LB 9/1995)

a	b	c
d	e	f
g	h	i
j	k	l

Upper Case Alphabet (LB 9/1995)

C	B	A
F	E	D
I	H	G
L	K	J

Lower Case Alphabet (LB 9/1995)

m	n	o
p	q	r
s	t	u
v	w	x

Upper Case Alphabet (LB 9/1995)

O	N	M
R	Q	P
U	T	S
X	W	V

Lower Case Alphabet (LB 9/1995)

y	z	period ●
question mark	exclamation point	quotation mark
?	!	"

Making-up Words

1. Use the alphabet to identify the name of each letter and the sound that it makes.

2. Use the alphabet to make-up words as many as you can.
Example: (**beautiful**)
a e l b f l t u u
at bat fat
ate bate fate late
it bit bite fit lit
eat beat feat tea teal

(continued)
be bet let but blue
fib lute flute flue

3. Use the alphabet to spell words.

4. Use the alphabet to trace or write the letters.

Upper Case Alphabet (LB 9/1995)

	Z	**Y**
The upper case alphabet is arranged so that it will match the lower case alphabet when making a double sided copy.		

Letter/Sound and Writing Practice (LB 9/1995)

Aa	Bb	Cc	Dd	Ee	Ff
Gg	Hh	Ii	Jj	Kk	Ll
Mm	Nn	Oo	Pp	Qq	Rr
Ss	Tt	Uu	Vv	Ww	Xx
Yy	Zz	0 Mistake **Mastery**	1 Mistake **Pass**	2 Mistakes **Retest**	3+ Mistakes **No Pass**

1. Circle each letter the child missed in naming the letters and its sounds.
2. Write the letter/s missed by the child in the appropriate box.
3. Have the child write the alphabet. Copy the letters above. Practice naming the letters and its corresponding sound in random. (This is not an assessment).

Name: Date

School:

Letter/Sound and Writing Practice (LB 9/1995)

Letter/Sound, Spelling, & Reading/Writing Practice (LB 6/2005)

Aa apple	**Bb** bee	**Cc** celery	**Dd** deer	**Ee** eagle	**Ff** feather
Gg giraffe	**Hh** house	**Ii** iron	**Jj** jar	**Kk** kite	**Ll** lion
Mm moon	**Nn** nine	**Oo** oyster	**Pp** pencil	**Qq** queen	**Rr** rabbit
Ss snake	**Tt** teeth	**Uu** unicorn	**Vv** vase	**Ww** wig	**Xx** x-ray

Yy yo-yo	**Zz** zipper	Name: Date
		1. Read the letter. Say the sound. 2. Spell the word. Read word in parts. Sound out the word. 3. Read the word (three times). Write the word in the box.

Picture/Word Recognition (LB 6/2004)

Aa ant

Liliaburton@aol.com
LOB Educational Services (6/2004)

Aa apple

Liliaburton@aol.com
LOB Educational Services (6/2004)

Aa alligator

Liliaburton@aol.com
LOB Educational Services (6/2004)

Bb ball

Liliaburton@aol.com
LOB Educational Services (6/2004)

Bb bubble

Liliaburton@aol.com
LOB Educational Services (6/2004)

Bb bumblebee

Liliaburton@aol.com
LOB Educational Services (6/2004)

Cc cat
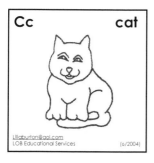
Liliaburton@aol.com
LOB Educational Services (6/2004)

Cc crayon

Liliaburton@aol.com
LOB Educational Services (6/2004)

Cc cantaloupe
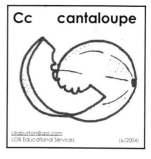
Liliaburton@aol.com
LOB Educational Services (6/2004)

Dd dog

Liliaburton@aol.com
LOB Educational Services (6/2004)

Dd doctor

Liliaburton@aol.com
LOB Educational Services (6/2004)

Dd dinosaur

Liliaburton@aol.com
LOB Educational Services (6/2004)

Reading Sentences (LB 3/2004)

Aa

An <u>alligator</u> looks like a crocodile.

Aa

Henry likes the red ripe juicy <u>apple</u>.

Aa

An <u>ant</u> is a bug.

Bb

Watch out for the huge <u>bumblebee.</u>

Bb

My mother and I blew <u>bubbles</u> in the yard.

Bb

The <u>ball</u> rolled across the street.

Cc

I like cold sweet <u>cantaloupe</u> for a snack.

Cc

Ned colored his drawing with <u>crayons</u>.

Cc

The <u>cat</u> ran after the little mouse.

Dd

<u>Dinosaurs</u> no longer roam the earth.

Dd

The <u>doctor</u> prescribed medicine for coughing.

Dd

My neighbor's <u>dog</u> barked all night.

Picture/Word Recognition (LB 3/2004)

Ee egg	**Ee** eagle	**Ee** envelope
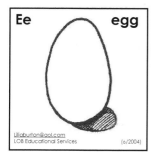		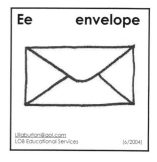
Liliaburton@aol.com LOB Educational Services (6/2004)	Liliaburton@aol.com LOB Educational Services (6/2004)	Liliaburton@aol.com LOB Educational Services (6/2004)
Ff fan	**Ff** flashlight	**Ff** fortune teller
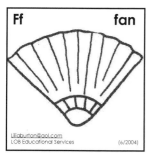		
Liliaburton@aol.com LOB Educational Services (6/2004)	Liliaburton@aol.com LOB Educational Services (6/2004)	Liliaburton@aol.com LOB Educational Services (6/2004)
Gg grapes	**Gg** guitar	**Gg** gorilla

Liliaburton@aol.com LOB Educational Services (6/2004)	Liliaburton@aol.com LOB Educational Services (6/2004)	Liliaburton@aol.com LOB Educational Services (6/2004)
Hh house	**Hh** hammer	**Hh** hamburger
	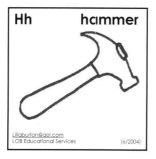	
Liliaburton@aol.com LOB Educational Services (6/2004)	Liliaburton@aol.com LOB Educational Services (6/2004)	Liliaburton@aol.com LOB Educational Services (6/2004)

Reading Sentences (LB 3/2004)

Ee
Don't forget to write the address on the <u>envelope</u>.

Ee
The <u>eagle</u> flew high in the sky.

Ee
I would like a scrambled <u>egg</u> for breakfast.

Ff
The <u>fortune teller</u> told me that I would find my lost key.

Ff
Grandpa uses a <u>flashlight</u> when it is dark.

Ff
I turn the <u>fan</u> on when the weather is hot.

Gg
Max saw a big <u>gorilla</u> at the zoo.

Gg
Dad plays his <u>guitar</u> as he sings a lullaby.

Gg
<u>Grapes</u> are sweet fruits.

Hh
Some people like <u>hamburgers</u> better than hotdogs.

Hh
You need a <u>hammer</u> and nails to build a clubhouse.

Hh
Grandma's <u>house</u> is cool during summer.

Picture/Word Recognition (LB 3/2004)

Ii ink 	Ii igloo 	Ii ice cream cone 
Jj jar 	Jj jacket 	Jj jack-o-lantern 
Kk kite 	Kk kayak 	Kk kangaroo 
Ll lamp 	Ll light bulb 	Ll limousine 

Liliaburton@aol.com
LOB Educational Services (6/2004)

Reading Sentences (LB 3/2004)

Ii You put scoops of ice cream in the <u>ice cream cone.</u>	**Ii** Have you ever slept in an <u>igloo</u>?	**Ii** Write your name in black <u>ink</u>.
Jj I will make a <u>jack-o-lantern</u> for Halloween.	**Jj** Sol wears his <u>jacket</u> when he gets cold.	**Jj** Najida has a <u>jar</u> full of coins.
Kk A <u>kangaroo</u> is found in Australia.	**Kk** My family went to a <u>kayak</u> expedition	**Kk** My friend and I flew a <u>kite</u> in the park last Saturday.
Ll The star of the show arrived in a <u>limousine</u>.	**Ll** Mom needs a brighter <u>light bulb</u> so she can see.	**Ll** Grandpa needs a new bulb for the <u>lamp</u>.

Picture/Word Recognition (LB 3/2004)

Mm man 	**Mm** mirror 	**Mm** microphone 
Nn nest 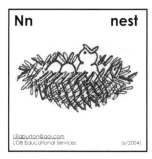	**Nn** necklace 	**Nn** nutcracker 
Oo one 	**Oo** orange 	**Oo** octopus 
Pp pot 	**Pp** pencil 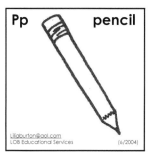	**Pp** pineapple 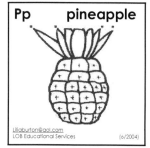

Liliaburton@aol.com
LOB Educational Services   (6/2004)

Reading Sentences (LB 3/2004)

Mm
The judge used a <u>microphone</u> to announce the winner.

Mm
Najida likes to look at herself on a large <u>mirror</u>.

Mm
The <u>man</u> was surprised to find a bag of money in his car.

Nn
You crack a nut shell with a <u>nutcracker</u>.

Nn
My mother gave me a pearl <u>necklace</u>.

Nn
Kwisi found ten eggs in the <u>nest</u>.

Oo
An <u>octopus</u> has many arms.

Oo
I like to drink a cup of <u>orange</u> juice in the morning.

Oo
I have <u>one</u> more day to rest before I go back to work.

Pp
A <u>pineapple</u> is a famous fruit in Hawaii.

Pp
Kwisi wrote a letter to his grandma with a <u>pencil</u>.

Pp
Grandpa boiled hotdogs in a <u>pot</u>.

Picture/Word Recognition (LB 3/2004)

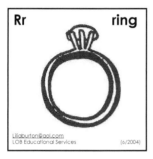

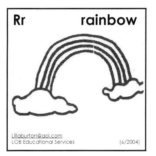

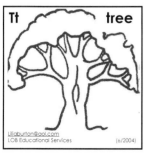

Reading Sentences (LB 3/2004)

Qq End your asking sentence with a <u>question mark.</u>	**Qq** There are four <u>quarters</u> in a dollar.	**Qq** The <u>queen</u> invited guest to perform at the festival.
Rr The <u>rocking chair</u> is my mom's favorite chair.	**Rr** Is there really a pot of gold at the end of a <u>rainbow</u>?	**Rr** Najida's <u>ring</u> is designed like flowers.
Ss There is a <u>sunflower</u> growing in the backyard.	**Ss** A <u>starfish</u> is a sea animal with five arms.	**Ss** The <u>sun</u> is the closest star to earth.
Tt The <u>telephone</u> rang loudly.	**Tt** The <u>turtle</u> walked slowly to the pond.	**Tt** We sat under a <u>tree</u> while we counted the stars.

Picture/Word Recognition (LB 3/2004)

Uu urn  Liliaburton@aol.com / LOB Educational Services (6/2004)	**Uu** unicorn  Liliaburton@aol.com / LOB Educational Services (6/2004)	**Uu** umbrella  Liliaburton@aol.com / LOB Educational Services (6/2004)
Vv vase  Liliaburton@aol.com / LOB Educational Services (6/2004)	**Vv** vacuum 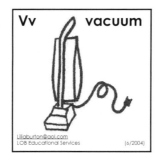 Liliaburton@aol.com / LOB Educational Services (6/2004)	**Vv** vegetables 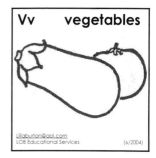 Liliaburton@aol.com / LOB Educational Services (6/2004)
Ww watch  Liliaburton@aol.com / LOB Educational Services (6/2004)	**Ww** wagon  Liliaburton@aol.com / LOB Educational Services (6/2004)	**Ww** watermelon  Liliaburton@aol.com / LOB Educational Services (6/2004)
Xx ox  Liliaburton@aol.com / LOB Educational Services (6/2004)	**Xx** x-ray 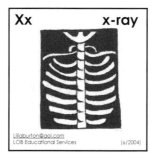 Liliaburton@aol.com / LOB Educational Services (6/2004)	**Xx** xylophone  Liliaburton@aol.com / LOB Educational Services (6/2004)

Reading Sentences (LB 3/2004)

Uu
The weather forecaster predicted rain, so bring your <u>umbrella.</u>

Uu
I have never seen a real <u>unicorn</u>.

Uu
Rina found an <u>urn</u> in her aunt's basement.

Vv
<u>Vegetables</u> are good and healthy foods to eat.

Vv
My mother hired a maid to <u>vacuum</u> our house.

Vv
Kim put the roses in the <u>vase.</u>

Ww
Is <u>watermelon</u> a sweet juicy vegetable or fruit?

Ww
The children rode to the farm in a <u>wagon</u>.

Ww
My <u>watch</u> indicates that it is now twelve o'clock.

Xx
He played beautiful music with a <u>xylophone</u>

Xx
My grandma had an <u>x-ray</u> of her knee.

Xx
An <u>ox</u> is a good animal for food or farming.

Picture/Word Recognition (LB 3/2004)

Yy yarn	Yy yo-yo	Yy yardstick

Zz zoo	Zz zipper	Zz zucchini
	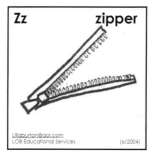	

First Reading	Second Reading	Third Reading
Number of words .... _78_	Number of words .... _78_	Number of words ...... _78_
Errors .... ___	Errors .... ___	Errors .... ___
Words read correctly ... ___	Words read correctly ... ___	Words read correctly .. ___

Reading Intervention

1. Read the letter. Identify the picture.
2. Spell the word.
3. Sound out the word.
4. Read the word.
5. Read the word in parts (for multi-syllabic words only).
6. Blend the parts smoothly and read the word (for multi-syllabic only).
7. Practice reading the words at least three times (3X)

Reading Sentences (LB 3/2004)

Yy
Sol measured the length of the room with a <u>yardstick</u>.

Yy
Kwisi won first prize in a <u>yo-yo</u> competition.

Yy
Najidah used red <u>yarn</u> to knit a sweater.

Zz
I like to eat fried <u>zucchini</u> with fried chicken.

Zz
The old traveling bag needs a new <u>zipper</u>.

Zz
You see many different kinds of animals at the <u>zoo</u>.

First Reading

1. Read each word in a sentence.
2. If you have difficulty in reading a word, sound it out then say the word.

Second Reading

1. Read two or three words at a time.
2. Blend the words together, smoothly to the end of each sentence.

Third Reading

1. Read each sentence smoothly.
2. Ask who or what is the subject in the sentence.
3. Ask what is being said about the subject.

Note

This page has been arranged so that the sentences will correspond or match the pictures and words for double sided copy.

Letter/Sound, Spelling, and Sight Words (1997, Redesigned 2005)

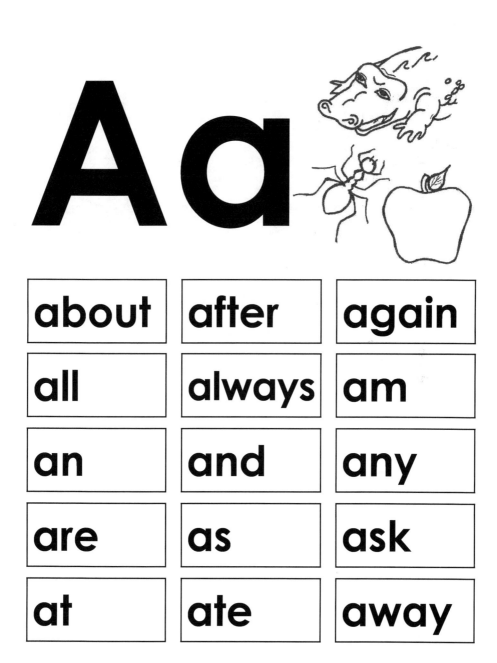

about	after	again
all	always	am
an	and	any
are	as	ask
at	ate	away

Letter/Sound, Spelling, and Sight Words (1997, Redesigned 2005)

Bb

be	because	been
beep	before	best
better	big	black
blue	both	bring
brown	but	butter

Letter/Sound, Spelling, and Sight Words (1997, Redesigned 2005)

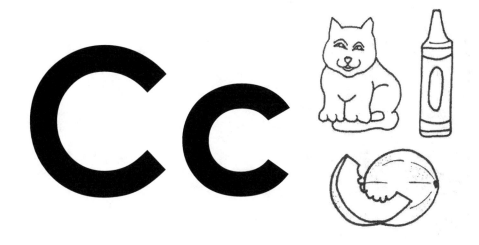

call	came	can
crack	clean	cold
come	cost	could
crack	crawl	create
cross	cry	cut

Letter/Sound, Spelling, and Sight Words (1997, Redesigned 2005)

dent	did	died
dig	dive	do
does	done	don't
down	drawn	dread
dried	drive	drown

Letter/Sound, Spelling, and Sight Words (1997, Redesigned 2005)

ear	earn	eat
eight	end	ending
enjoy	enter	entrance
erase	errand	even
ever	every	exit

Letter/Sound, Spelling, and Sight Words (1997, Redesigned 2005)

fall	**far**	**fast**
fat	**fill**	**find**
first	**five**	**fly**
for	**found**	**four**
from	**full**	**funny**

Letter/Sound, Spelling, and Sight Words (1997, Redesigned 2005)

Gg

gave	get	give
go	goes	going
got	grade	gray
greet	grin	grind
grow	growing	grown

Letter/Sound, Spelling, and Sight Words (1997, Redesigned 2005)

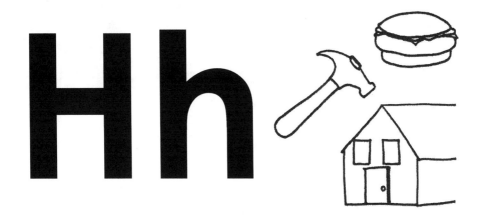

had	harm	has
have	he	help
her	here	him
his	hold	hot
how	hunt	hurt

Letter/Sound, Spelling, and Sight Words (1997, Redesigned 2005)

ice	icicles	if
illustrate	in	indoor
inside	intent	intern
into	invite	is
island	it	its

Letter/Sound, Spelling, and Sight Words (1997, Redesigned 2005)

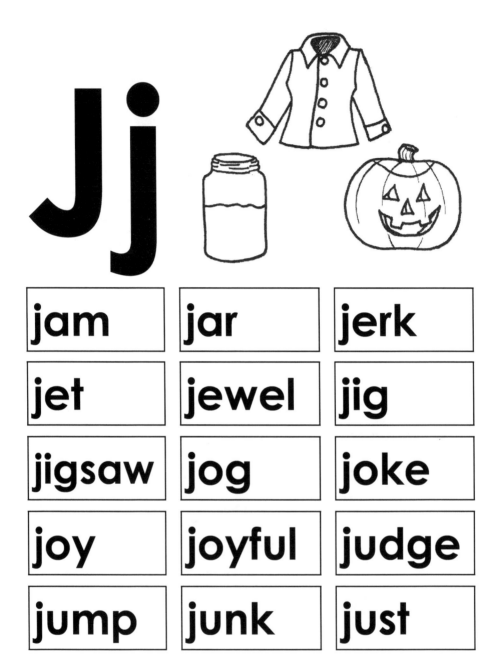

jam	jar	jerk
jet	jewel	jig
jigsaw	jog	joke
joy	joyful	judge
jump	junk	just

Letter/Sound, Spelling, and Sight Words (1997, Redesigned 2005)

keep	kin	kind
kindly	kite	knee
knife	knight	knock
knocked	knocking	know
knowing	known	kraft

Letter/Sound, Spelling, and Sight Words (1997, Redesigned 2005)

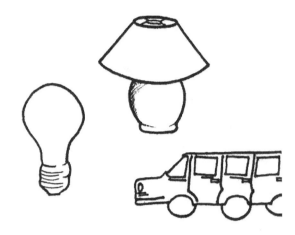

land	landed	lean
learn	let	light
like	line	listen
little	live	long
look	loop	low

Letter/Sound, Spelling, and Sight Words (1997, Redesigned 2005)

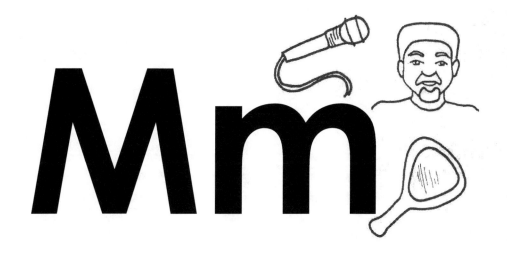

mad	made	make
man	many	mark
may	me	mean
more	most	much
must	my	myself

Letter/Sound, Spelling, and Sight Words (1997, Redesigned 2005)

name	neat	need
never	new	next
nice	night	no
nod	none	not
note	now	nun

Letter/Sound, Spelling, and Sight Words (1997, Redesigned 2005)

odor	of	old
on	once	one
only	open	or
order	our	out
over	owe	own

Letter/Sound, Spelling, and Sight Words (1997, Redesigned 2005)

pack	paid	pain
pane	pay	pick
pin	play	please
power	praise	pretty
pull	push	put

Letter/Sound, Spelling, and Sight Words (1997, Redesigned 2005)

quack	quail	quart
queen	question	quick
quiet	quill	quilt
quit	quite	quiver
quiz	quotation	quote

Letter/Sound, Spelling, and Sight Words (1997, Redesigned 2005)

rain	ran	ray
read	red	ride
right	ring	rise
rock	rode	rose
row	ruin	run

Letter/Sound, Spelling, and Sight Words (1997, Redesigned 2005)

sad	said	saw
say	see	shall
she	shop	show
sin	sing	sit
sleep	soon	stop

Letter/Sound, Spelling, and Sight Words (1997, Redesigned 2005)

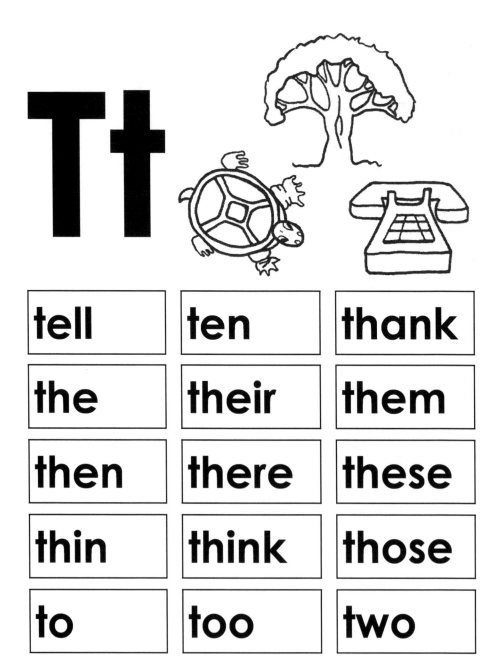

tell	ten	thank
the	their	them
then	there	these
thin	think	those
to	too	two

Letter/Sound, Spelling, and Sight Words (1997, Redesigned 2005)

ugly	ulcer	umpire
under	undo	unite
unity	untie	up
upon	upper	us
usage	use	utility

Letter/Sound, Spelling, and Sight Words (1997, Redesigned 2005)

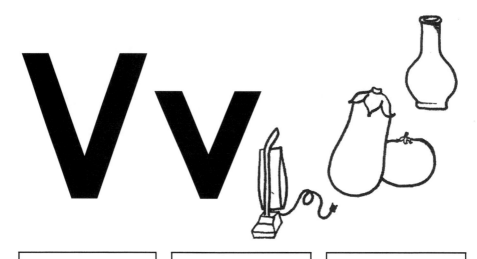

vacant	vacuum	vain
value	valve	van
vane	vapor	varied
vault	veil	verb
very	vice	vinegar

Letter/Sound, Spelling, and Sight Words (1997, Redesigned 2005)

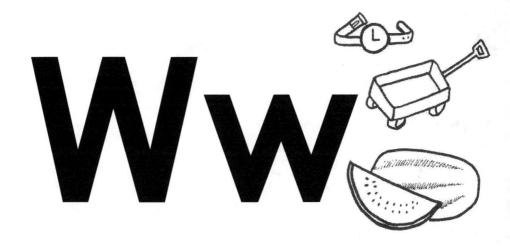

want	warn	was
we	well	went
were	what	when
where	white	who
why	will	wish

Letter/Sound, Spelling, and Sight Words (1997, Redesigned 2005)

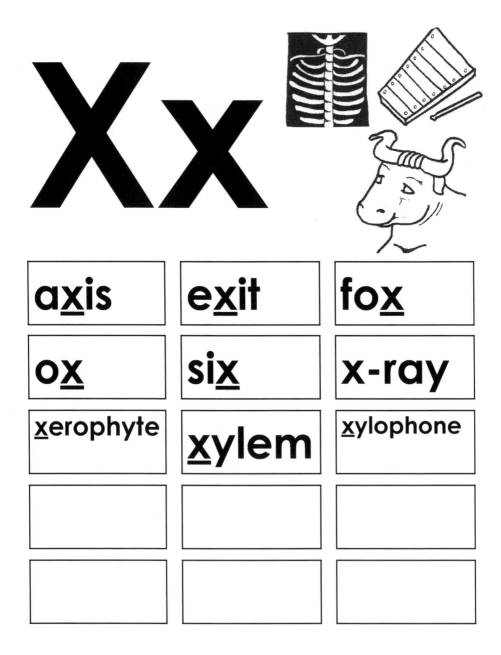

a<u>x</u>is	e<u>x</u>it	fo<u>x</u>
o<u>x</u>	si<u>x</u>	x-ray
<u>x</u>erophyte	<u>x</u>ylem	<u>x</u>ylophone

Letter/Sound, Spelling, and Sight Words (1997, Redesigned 2005)

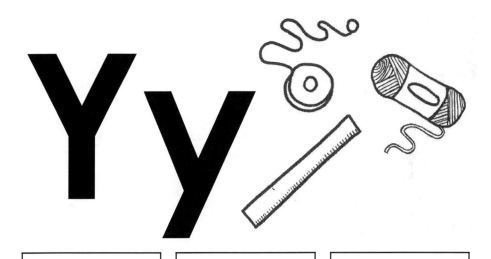

yak	yam	yank
yard	yarn	year
yell	yellow	yes
yoke	you	your
yo-yo	yuck	yummy

Letter/Sound, Spelling, and Sight Words (1997, Redesigned 2005)

zap	zeal	zebra
zero	zest	zigzag
zip	zipper	zodiac
zone	zoo	zookeeper
zoology	zoom	zucchini

Word Wheel **Manipulative Diagram**

(Patent Appl. No.29/189, 246)

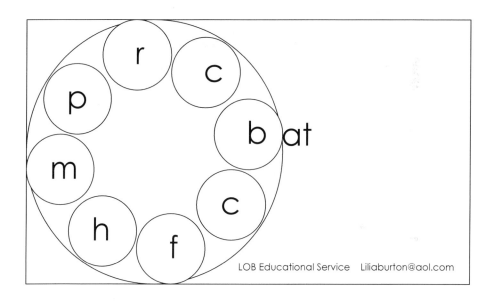

LOB Educational Service   Liliaburton@aol.com

For information, call: telephone # 334 281-1582 or email: lb217@bellsouth.com

Note: This diagram is similar to the actual *Word Wheel* manipulative materials being used in my classroom. *Word Wheel* manipulative materials consist of letters that make rhyming words. A circle with eight different letters is attached to a card with a paper fastener in order to allow rotation. Each time the wheel rotates and each letter aligns with the letters on the card, a rhyming word is formed. It focuses on developing skills such as recognizing sounds and putting together individual sounds to make spoken words. The purpose of using *Word Wheel* is to practice reading text accurately and quickly. *Word Wheel* is teacher created materials based on the concept of hands-on learning by Vygotsky (1986) and his cultural-historical theory of learning. This hands-on learning is also based on Dewey's (2005) constructivist theory referring to students learning as a group or individually as they construct meaning in a way that makes sense. This manipulative is designed to encourage cooperative learning and interactive work in the classroom or at home.

References:

Dewey, J. (2005). Democracy and education: An introduction to the philosophy of education. New York, NY. Cosimo, Inc.

Vygotsky, L. (1986). (revised and edited by Kozulin, A.). Thought and language. The Massachusetts Institute of Technology, Cambridge, Massachusetts. The MIT Press.

Word Wheel (Manipulative) Skills

Cards & Wheels	Letter Blending	Phonics and Spelling Skills (Sounds/Rhymes)	Cards & Wheels	Letter Blending	Phonics and Spelling Skills (Sounds/Rhymes)
1	ace	Words with long a	31	in	Words with short i
2	age	Words with long a	32	ine	Words with long i
3	ack	Words with short a	33	ing	Words with ing
4	ake	Words with long a	34	ink	Words with short i
5	ad	Words with short a	35	it	Words with short i
6	ade	Words with long a	36	ite	Words with long i
7	ag	Words with short a	37	oke	Words with long o
8	ag	Words with short a	38	ook	Words with oo
9	ale	Words with long a	39	on	Words with short o
10	all	Words with short a	40	one	Words with long o
11	am	Words with short a	41	ong	Words with ong
12	ame	Words with long a	42	ood	Words with oo
13	an	Words with short a	43	ow	Words like ou (cloud)
14	ane	Words with long a	44	ow	Words like though
15	ar	Words with ar	45	ox	Words with short o
16	are	Words with long a	46	oy	Words like oi (boil)
17	at	Words with short a	47	ub	Words with short u
18	ate	Words with long a	48	uck	Words with short u
19	ate	Words with long a	49	ud	Words with short u
20	ave	Words with long a	50	ude	Words with long u
21	ay	Words with long a	51	ug	Words with short u
22	ay	Words with long a	52	um	Words with short u
23	eat	Words with ea (ee)	53	un	Words with short u
24	ee	Words with ee	54	une	Words with long u
25	en	Words with short e	55	ung	Words with ung
26	et	Words with short e	56	unk	Words with short u
27	ick	Words with short i	57	ur	Words with controlled r
28	ig	Words with short i	58	ure	Words with long u
29	im	Words with short i	59	ut	Words with short u
30	ime	Words with long i	60	ute	Words with long u

1. Point at the letters on the card. **Say:** _"These letters say the rime_ . . . .(ex: at). _Spell the rime. Let's sound it out. Read the rime."_
2. Point at each letter on the wheel. **Say:** _"What letter is this? What is the sound of this letter?"_
3. **Say:** _"Let's read some words with the same rime."_ Rotate the wheel and align each letter with the letters on the card. **Say:** _Let's sound it out_ . . . . (ex: b/a/t)._Read the word_ . . . . (ex: bat).

Word Wheel Manipulative Practice/Drill
(patent appl. No.29/189,246)

Rimes	Letter/Word Combinations								
1. ace	face	lace	mace	pace	place	race	space	trace		
2. age	cage	gage	page	rage	sage	stage	wage			
3. ack	back	hack	jack	lack	pack	smack	snack	stack	track	
4. ake	bake	cake	fake	lake	make	rake	sake	stake	rake	wake
5. ad	bad	dad	fad	had	lad	mad	pad	sad		
6. ade	bade	fade	jade	made	shade	trade	wade			
7. ag	bag	hag	jag	lag	mag	nag	rag	sag		
8. ag	shag	snag	swag	tag	wag					
9. ale	bale	dale	gale	hale	male	pale	sale	stale	tale	
10. all	ball	call	fall	gall	hall	mall	small	stall	tall	wall
11. am	cam	dam	jam	ham	lam	pam	ram	sam	tam	
12. ame	came	dame	fame	game	lame	name	same	tame		
13. an	ban	can	fan	man	pan	ran	tan	van		
14. ane	bane	cane	jane	lane	mane	pane	sane	vane		
15. ar	bar	car	far	jar	par	scar	star	tar	war	
16. are	bare	care	dare	fare	hare	mare	rare	spare	stare	
17. at	bat	cat	fat	hat	mat	pat	rat	sat	stat	
18. ate	bate	date	fate	gate	grate	hate	kate	late		
19. ate	mate	rate	skate	slate	state					
20. ave	brave	cave	dave	gave	grace	pave	rave	save	shave	wave
21. ay	say	day	gay	hay	kay	may	pay			
22. ay	pray	ray	say	spray	stray	tray	way			
23. eat	beat	feat	heat	meat	neat	repeat	seat			
24. ee	bee	gee	knee	see	spree	tee	thee	three	tree	
25. en	ben	den	hen	men	pen	ten	wren	yen		
26. et	bet	get	jet	let	pet	set	vet	wet	yet	
27. ick	brick	click	lick	nick	prick	rick	sick	slick	trick	
28. ig	big	dig	fig	gig	jig	pig	rig	twig	wig	zig
29. im	brim	dim	grim	him	jim	rim	sim	slim	swim	trim
30. ime	crime	grime	lime	mime	prime	rime	slime	time		
31. in	bin	fin	gin	kin	pin	sin	spin	tin	twin	win
32. ine	dine	fine	line	mine	pine	shine	spine	swine	wine	whine
33. ing	bring	king	ping	ring	sing	sting	string	wing	wring	
34. ink	blink	brink	drink	link	mink	pink	sink	stink	think	wink
35. it	bit	fit	hit	kit	knit	omit	pit	sit	skit	wit
36. ite	bite	kite	lite	mite	nite	rite	site	spite	white	write
37. oke	broke	coke	joke	poke	spoke	stroke	woke	yoke		
38. ook	book	brook	cook	crook	hook	look	nook	shook	took	
39. on	con	don	neon	son	ton	won	yon			
40. one	bone	cone	clone	krone	lone	shone	strone	throne	tone	zone

41. ong	bong	dong	fong	gong	long	prong	song	tong	throng	wrong
42. ood	brood	food	good	hood	mood	stood	wood			
43. ow	bow	cow	how	now	pow	prow	wow			
44. ow	bow	crow	grow	know	low	mow	row	sow	throw	tow
45. ox	box	fox	lox	pox	sox					
46. oy	boy	coy	joy	ploy	roy	soy	toy	troy		
47. ub	cub	club	dub	flub	nub	pud	rud	sud	stud	tud
48. uck	buck	duck	guck	luck	muck	puck	suck	stuck	tuck	yuck
49. ud	bud	cud	dud	fud	mud	pud	rud	stud	thud	
50. ude	dude	crude	elude	exude	include	jude	nude	rude		
51. ug	bug	dug	drug	hug	jug	mug	rug	snug	tug	
52. um	bum	drum	hum	mum	rum	sum	slum	strum		
53. un	bun	dun	fun	gun	nun	run	sun	shun	stun	tun
54. une	attune	dune	immune	june	prune	rune	tune			
55. ung	bung	dung	hung	rung	sung	stung	strung	swung	wrung	
56. unk	bunk	dunk	drunk	funk	hunk	junk	punk	sunk	skunk	trunk
57. ur	bur	blur	cur	fur	femur	slur	spur			
58. ure	cure	ensure	insure	lure	manure	mature	pure			
59. ut	but	cut	gut	hut	nut	rut	shut			
60. ute	brute	cute	dilute	flute	jute	lute	mute	tribute		

Choosing Good Manipulatives

Manipulatives in reading should provide:

1. Appropriate text for the child's age and reading level.
2. Pictures should be clear and labeled.
3. Designs should be colorful or interesting for the child's pleasure and fun.
4. Phonological awareness skill practice.
5. Letters/sounds should add new words to the child's vocabulary.

Brooks, M. & Engmann-Hartung, D. (1976). *Pro.ed. Pad (#1079)*. Austin, Texas

Manipulatives should promote the following areas of early childhood development:

1. **Cognitive and literacy development** including recognition of rhymes, blending and segmenting syllables, recognizing initial sounds of spoken words. In addition, letter sound recognition, symbolic

representation, adding/deleting/substituting letters and order relationships should be included.

2. **Social and emotional development** including cooperation, expressing pride and confidence in a cooperative learning, small group instruction or partner learning.

3. **Physical development** including coordination of small muscles and eye-hand movements as well as sense of rhythm and quickness.

4. **Personal development** including creative expression, self-discovery, self-esteem, and satisfaction in academic achievement.

Blankenship, T. (2003). *Wyoming early childhood readiness standards.* Wyoming Department of Education. Cheyene, WY.

Synonyms, Antonyms, Homophones, and Compound Words

(Word Wheel Manipulatives) For information: Call telephone # 334 281-1582 or email: lb217@bellsouth.com

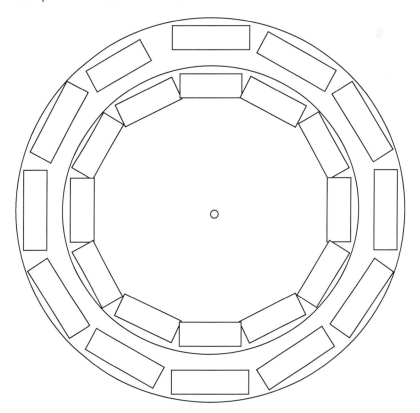

* Each box represents a word. This is only an example.

- Connect the small wheel and the big wheel together with a paper fastener, (small wheel on top).
- Rotate the small wheel to correctly match the synonyms, antonyms, homophones, or compound words.
- Use each word in a sentence for vocabulary and comprehension.

Synonyms

Word Wheel #1

1. beautiful — pretty
2. below — under
3. big — large
4. build — make
5. clean — neat
6. close — shut
7. dad — father
8. dark — dim
9. end — finish
10. erase — cancel
11. few — some
12. good — nice

Word Wheel #2

1. halt — stop
2. hold — retain
3. live — survive
4. look — watch
5. mean — wicked
6. night — evening
7. put — place
8. small — little
9. smart — sharp
10. tall — high
11. upper — higher
12. wild — unruly

Word Wheel #3

1. begin — start
2. come — arrive
3. divide — part
4. go — leave
5. hate — dislike
6. like — prefer
7. open — ajar
8. pain — ache
9. quick — fast
10. rest — relax
11. silent — quiet
12. wreck — ruin

Antonyms

Word Wheel #4

1. aunt — uncle
2. black — white
3. close — open
4. come — go
5. dark — bright
6. earn — spend
7. fall — rise
8. false — true
9. female — male
10. few — many
11. good — bad
12. hold — drop

Word Wheel #5

1. king — queen
2. like — hate
3. low — high
4. little — big
5. live — die
6. man — woman
7. mother — father
8. nice — mean
9. old — new
10. own — rent
11. pretty — ugly
12. pull — push

Word Wheel #6

1. sell — buy
2. short — long
3. small — large
4. take — give
5. tall — short
6. upper — lower
7. weak — strong
8. well — ill
9. wild — tame
10. work — rest
11. yes — no
12. zip — unzip

Homophones

Word Wheel #7

1. blue — blew
2. by, buy — bye
3. dear — deer
4. eight — ate
5. eye — I
6. flower — flour
7. four — for
8. hear — here
9. knew — new
10. know — no
11. one — won

Word Wheel #8

1. pail — pale
2. pain — pane
3. red — read
4. right — write
5. sail — sale
6. sea — see
7. so — saw, sew
8. son — sun
9. tail — tale
10. their — there
11. too — to, two

Word Wheel #9

1. dew — due
2. die — dye
3. eyes — ice
4. fair — fare
5. hair — hare
6. mail — male
7. meat — meet
8. pair — pare
9. tea — tee
10. weight — wait
11. would — wood

Compound Words
Word Wheel #10

1. any	thing
2. bed	room
3. blow	hole
4. blue	berry
5. boy	friend
6. break	fast
7. door	knob
8. drug	store
9. earth	worm
10. ever	green
11. fire	place

Word Wheel #11

1. flower	pot
2. fruit	cake
3. girl	friend
4. grass	hopper
5. hair	line
6. hand	some
7. handy	man
8. head	ache
9. home	work
10. house	fly
11. house	hold

Word Wheel #12

1. in	tend
2. in	land
3. knock	out
4. north	east
5. north	west
6. out	post
7. over	grown
8. land	slide
9. lake	shore
10. light	house
11. moon	light

Compound Words
Word Wheel #13

1. photo	graph
2. play	house
3. police	man
4. plum	age
5. rain	drop
6. rest	room
7. sail	boat
8. sales	person
9. screen	play
10. sea	horse
11. sea	shell

Word Wheel #14

1. see	saw
2. some	thing
3. some	times
4. sun	shine
5. side	walk
6. to	day
7. tooth	ache
8. tooth	brush
9. tooth	paste
10. under	water
11. waste	basket

Word Wheel #15

1. use	less
2. win	chill
3. wind	pipe
4. wind	shield
5. with	draw
6. with	out
7. wonder	land
8. work	book
9. work	out
10. yard	stick
11. zoo	keeper

Vocabulary and Comprehension

(Selected Nouns, 1997)

Selected Nouns is a collection of nouns, pictures, and word meanings made easy for beginner readers, K-3. The information collected in this book is designed to improve students' reading skills. First, it helps children develop their phonological awareness skill through letter/sound recognition and picture association. According to research, pictures and definitions improve students' ability too recall stated meanings and details. In addition, *Selected Nouns* is used as a reading resource in phonics instruction such as letter-sound association, letter-picture relationship, initial and ending sound-symbol, and spelling as well as segmenting and blending. Next, *Selected Nouns* is used to improve oral reading fluency by practice reading and rereading the words and sentences. Word study skills such as sight words, rhyming words, phonetic drills, homophones, synonyms/antonyms, and compound words enhance student' reading fluency. Then, *Selected Nouns* is used to enhance vocabulary by teaching explicitly both individual words and group of words in a sentence in order to understand the meaning of a particular word. The picture enhances the meaning of spoken words in a way that make sense. Finally, *Selected Nouns* is used to improve comprehension by identifying and asking questions about the picture and words that they read. By associating the pictures with the corresponding words or phrases, children can easily tell about what they just read when they are asked to retell what they understood and remembered.

Merriam Webster's Elementary Dictionary (1994). Merriam-Webster Inc.
The New Merriam-Webster Dictionary (1981). (Book ID 0-87779 900-8).
    Merriam-Webster Inc.

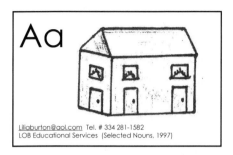

Aa

ap.art.ment   apartment

An apartment is a building occupied by more than one family.

Susan lives in an apartment.

Aa

al.li.ga.tor   alligator

An alligator is a large reptile with powerful jaws and a long tail that lives near water.

I have not seen an alligator

Aa

ap.ple   apple

An apple is a round sweet fruit. Most ripe apples are red, yellow and light green.

Joy brought a shiny red apple to his teacher yesterday.

Aa

aunt

An aunt is the sister of your father or mother.

My aunt Maria likes to watch television with my mother.

bank

A bank is a business that offers financial services for individuals or companies.

My money is safe in the bank.

bear

A bear is a four-legged furry animal with sharp claws and walks on the flat of its paws.

The big brown bear ran after the fox.

boy

A boy is a male child who grows up to be a man.

The little boy rode his little bike to town.

broom

A broom is a collection of twigs, bristles, or straws attached to a handle or stick.

I swept the floor with a broom.

Liliaburton@aol.com Tel. # 334 281-1582
LOB Educational Services (Selected Nouns, 1997)

cat

A cat is a domestic pet. Cats like to catch rats and mice.

The cat ran after a little gray mouse.

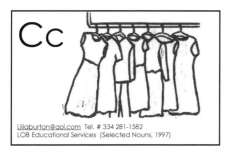

Liliaburton@aol.com Tel. # 334 281-1582
LOB Educational Services (Selected Nouns, 1997)

clo.set   **closet**

A closet is a small room in the house where you hang your clothes or store things.

My mother hangs her clothes in the closet.

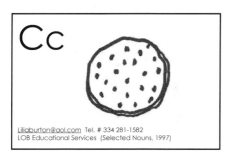

Liliaburton@aol.com Tel. # 334 281-1582
LOB Educational Services (Selected Nouns, 1997)

coo.kie   **cookie**

A cookie is a small flat crispy bake cake made from a sweetened dough.

Najida likes to bake oatmeal cookies.

Liliaburton@aol.com Tel. # 334 281-1582
LOB Educational Services (Selected Nouns, 1997)

cou.sin   **cousin**

A cousin is a child of your aunt or uncle.

My cousin Sam is coming to town.

dad

Dad is another name for father.

Her dad is the president of an investment company.

doll

A doll is a small toy that looks like a human being. Some dolls can talk or cry.

Linda wants a doll for her birthday.

dog

A dog is a pet animal. Dogs are related to foxes and wolves.

My neighbor's dog barked all night.

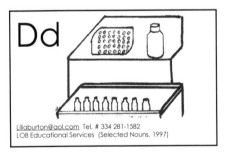

drugs.tore   drugstore

A drugstore is where over-the-counter or prescription drugs including snacks are sold.

He bought cough medicine from the drugstore.

ea.gle   **eagle**

An eagle is a large bird of prey with hooked bill, keen eyesight, and broad strong wings.

The bald eagle is the national bird of the United States.

earth

The earth is the third planet from the sun. We live on a planet called earth.

We grow plants and vegetables on planet earth.

en.gi.neer   **engineer**

An engineer is a person who operates an engine. Engineers work in a railroad train.

Florante's father is an engineer.

er.a.ser   **eraser**

An eraser is a rubber made to remove pencil writing. Erasers are found on some pencils.

Use an eraser to rewrite your sentence.

farm

A farm is a place to produce crops as well as raise and breed domestic animals.

My cousin Annie went on a field trip to a farm.

fa.ther   father

A father is a male parent. A father helps a mother support their family.

Jen's father is an engineer and her mother is a teacher.

flo.wer   flower

A flower grows on a plant. Flowers develop seeds that grow into new plants.

A rose is a kind of a flower.

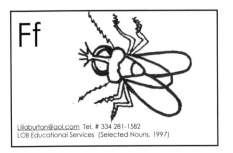

fly

A fly is a little two-winged insect. A common fly is called housefly. Flies fly around food.

A fly can spread few diseases.

gar.den   **garden**

A garden is a plot of land used to grow fruits, flowers, and vegetables.

<u>Joy had pretty flowers in her flower garden.</u>

gi.raffe   **giraffe**

A giraffe is the tallest land animal. A giraffe has a long neck and long legs.

<u>My friend and I saw a giraffe at the zoo last week.</u>

girl

A girl is a female child who grows up to be a woman. Your sister is a female child.

<u>The tall girl ran across the street.</u>

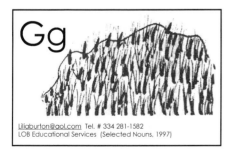

grass

A grass is a low green narrow—leaved plant that grows on lawns and farmlands.

<u>Cows and horses eat grass.</u>

han.dy.man   handyman

A handyman is a person who earns money by doing a variety of small jobs.

Mom needs a handyman to fix the bathroom door.

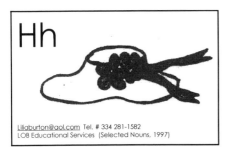

hat

A hat is worn on a head. Hats protect us from the sun, the rain, and the wind.

I wear hat to keep me cool in Summer.

hen

A hen is an adult female bird. A female chicken is a hen. Hens lay eggs.

Farmers grow hens for food.

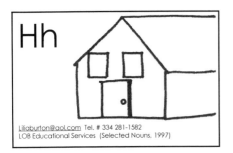

house

A house is a place where family lives. A house is found in the city or in the country.

My grandmother's house is in the country.

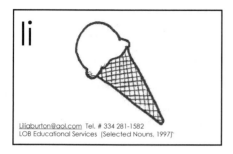

Ii

Liliaburton@aol.com Tel. # 334 281-1582
LOB Educational Services (Selected Nouns, 1997)

ice cream

An ice cream is smooth, sweet, and cold food eaten as a snack or a dessert.

Solomon's favorite dessert is vanilla ice cream.

Ii

Liliaburton@aol.com Tel. # 334 281-1582
LOB Educational Services (Selected Nouns, 1997)

il.lus.tra.tor   illustrator

An illustrator is a person who provides explanation by adding drawings, signs, or pictures in a story.

Kimberly is a good illustrator.

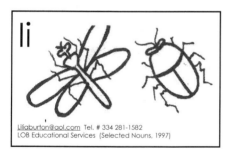

Ii

Liliaburton@aol.com Tel. # 334 281-1582
LOB Educational Services (Selected Nouns, 1997)

in.sect   insect

An insect is a small creature with six legs and a pair of wings. Flies, mosquitoes, and fleas are insects.

An insect is also called a bug.

Ii

Liliaburton@aol.com Tel. # 334 281-1582
LOB Educational Services (Selected Nouns, 1997)

is.land   island

An island is an area of land completely surrounded with water.

The State of Hawaii has many islands.

jack.al   **jackal**

A jackal is a doglike mammal. Jackals have long sharp fangs. Jackals eat small animals.

A jackal looks like a dog.

ja.ni.tor   **janitor**

A janitor is a person who attends to a cleaning or maintenance of a building.

Pedro's father is a janitor in an apartment building.

jaw

A jaw is the upper and lower bone that anchors the teeth that help you chew food.

My jaw is strong to chew meat.

jun.gle   **jungle**

A jungle is a land with thick overgrown tropical plants and vegetables.

A jungle is called tropical forest.

kan.ga.roo   **kangaroo**

A kangaroo is a large leaping animal with powerful hind legs, short forelegs, and a long tail.

A kangaroo carries its baby in its pocket.

kit.chen   **kitchen**

A kitchen is a part of a house where food is cooked. The kitchen is the best place to find food in the house.

My family eats in the kitchen.

kite

A kite is a light frame covered with cloth, paper or plastic. Kites are flown in the wind.

Kwisi flew his kite at the park.

knight

A knight is a man honored to serve a king or a queen. Knights live in Great Britain.

We say "Sir" to a British Knight.

law.yer   lawyer

A lawyer gives legal advices. A lawyer defends people in court or in other legal matters.

The lawyer who defended Art's case lived in New York.

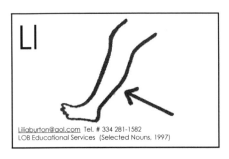

leg

A leg is a part of a body that helps a person to go on foot.

People have two legs while most animals have four legs.

li.on   lion

A lion is a large animal from Africa or northwest India. Lions have short tawny coat and tufted tail.

The hungry lion roared loudly.

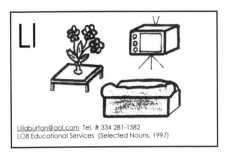

liv.ing room   living room

A living room is a place in your house intended for general social and leisure activities.

I watch T.V. in the living room.

meal

A meal is a food served and eaten in a serving. Some people eat three meals a day.

Dinner is the best time to eat a meal.

mom

Mom is another word for mother. Mom takes care of the house and children.

My mother washed and ironed my clothes.

monk.ey   monkey

A monkey is a long tailed medium sized primate. A baboon is in a monkey family.

The monkey jumped quickly from tree to tree.

moun.tain   mountain

A mountain is an earth elevated higher than a hill. Mountains have trees.

Pete climbed a high mountain.

nest

A nest is a bird's shelter made out of twigs, grass or things to hold its eggs and young.

There are nine eggs in the nest.

night craw.ler   night crawler

A night crawler is a large earthworm on the soil surface at night.

I saw a night crawler last night.

nurse

A nurse is a person trained to care for the sick or disabled.

The nurse at the hospital took my temperature.

nurs.er.y   nursery

A nursery is a room in a hospital where newborns stay and are cared for by medical staff.

Lorna's new baby sister is in the nursery.

of.fi.cer   officer

An officer is a person who is in charged with the enforcement of the law.

Officer Friendly keeps children safe at the traffic crossing.

or.ange   orange

An orange is a round or oval fruit of an orange tree, with a thick skin and juicy flesh.

My grandchildren drink fresh orange juice every morning.

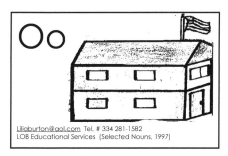

out.post   outpost

An outpost is a place for small military base in a remote area or in another country.

Sergeant Thomas works in an outpost in Japan.

owl

An owl has a large head with short hooked beak, large eyes set forward, and fluffy plumage.

The owl watched the full moon shining brightly last night.

paint.er   **painter**

A painter is a person who gets paid to paint either as an artist or a contract worker.

The painter painted my cousin's house red.

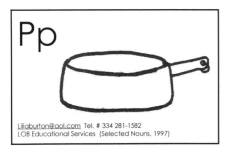

pan

A pan is a shallow, wide, open container used to hold liquid or for cooking.

The cooking pan is full of macaroni and cheese.

pa.ra.keet   **parakeet**

A parakeet is a small slender parrot. Parakeets have long tapering tails.

My pet parakeet flew out of its cage last Sunday morning.

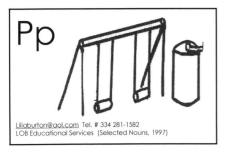

park

A park is a publicly owned area of land for public recreation such as playgrounds.

Solomon and Kwissy play basketball at the park.

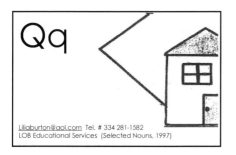

quad.ran.gle   quadrangle

A quadrangle is a four sided courtyard or enclosure. It is in an open rectangular yard.

People use the quadrangle for games or parties.

quail

A quail is a chicken-like bird. Quails have short tails, short wings, and stout bodies.

A quail is a small game bird from Europe.

queen

A queen is a wife or widow of a king. A queen is a woman who rules over a country.

Queen Elizabeth rules over the country of England.

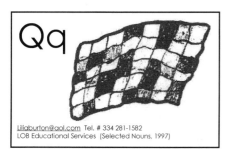

quilt

A quilt is a bed cover made of two layers of fabric stitched together with interior padding.

I use a quilt to keep me warm.

re.gis.trar　　　　　**registrar**

A registrar is a person in charge of official records in universities, city offices, and hospitals.

The registrar sent my college transcript to my new school.

res.tau.rant　　　　　**restaurant**

A restaurant is a place where meals are served to the public for a small charge.

My husband enjoys eating at a restaurant every Sunday.

rab.bit　　　　　**rabbit**

A rabbit is a small burrowing animal with long ears, soft fur, and a short tail.

Azubuike feeds carrots to his Pet rabbit.

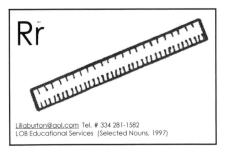

ru.ler　　　　　**ruler**

A ruler is a strip of wood, metal, or plastic used for drawing straight lines and measuring lengths.

Jen uses a ruler to measure pens.

Ss

Liliaburton@aol.com Tel. # 334 281-1582
LOB Educational Services (Selected Nouns, 1997)

sales.per.son   salesperson

A salesperson is a person who sells goods in the store or to outside customers.

Azubuike's friend works at the store as a salesperson.

Ss

Liliaburton@aol.com Tel. # 334 281-1582
LOB Educational Services (Selected Nouns, 1997)

scis.sor   scissor

A scissor is a hand-held cutting instrument made up of two crossed connected blades.

Najida's mother used scissors to cut the ribbon.

Ss

Liliaburton@aol.com Tel. # 334 281-1582
LOB Educational Services (Selected Nouns, 1997)

ser.vice sta.tion service station

A service station is a place where motor vehicles are repaired or gas filled.

I spent thirty dollars to fill up my gas tank at the service station.

Ss

Liliaburton@aol.com Tel. # 334 281-1582
LOB Educational Services (Selected Nouns, 1997)

snake

A snake is a legless scaly reptile with long tapering body. Some snakes are poisonous.

Mom said, "Watch out for snakes in the jungle".

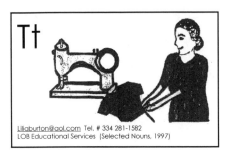

tai.lor   **tailor**

A tailor is a person who makes, repairs, and alters garments such as dresses and pants.

Sammy <u>took his pants to a tailor for alterations.</u>

tomb

A tomb is a place to put monuments to honor the deceased. A tomb is a place of burial.

<u>They</u> <u>carved his name on a tomb.</u>

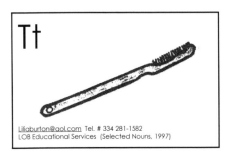

tooth.brush   **toothbrush**

A toothbrush is a brush used for cleaning teeth. You put toothpaste on your toothbrush.

<u>Kwisi</u> <u>brushes his teeth with a small toothbrush.</u>

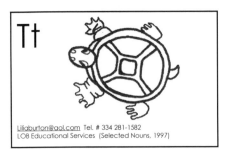

tur.tle   **turtle**

A turtle has a horny toothless jaw and a bony leathery shell. Turtles withdraw in their shells.

<u>Azu's pet turtle</u> <u>walked slowly to the pond.</u>

u.ku.le.le   **ukulele**

A ukulele is a small four stringed guitar. A ukulele is a musical instrument popular in Hawaii.

Maria knows how to play a ukulele.

un.cle   **uncle**

An uncle is a brother of your mother of father.

Joe's uncle plays a banjo while Maria plays a ukulele.

u.ni.corn   **unicorn**

A unicorn is a fabled creature represented as a horse with a single straight-spiraled horn.

Kim and Jen have seen a unicorn only on television.

u.niv.er.si.ty   **university**

A university is a place to earn a higher degree of education.

Sam, Cora, and Nancy took education courses at Alabama State University.

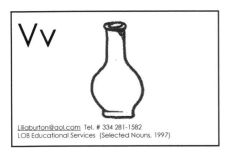

vase

A vase is usually tall and rounded open container used for displaying cut flowers.

My aunt put her vase on the table.

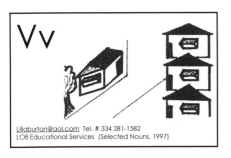

vil.lage   village

A village is a community smaller in population than own. Some United States cities

Uncle Bert's friend lives in a village.

ve.te.ri.na.ri.an   veterinarian

A veterinarian is a person qualified to treat injuries or diseases of animals.

The veterinarian took care of my dog's broken front legs.

vul.ture   vulture

A vulture is a large bird with dark plumage and a featherless head and neck.

A vulture flies over the mountain looking for food.

ware.house   **warehouse**

A warehouse is a place to store merchandise or goods for selling, buying or exchange.

The farm equipments are stored in the warehouse.

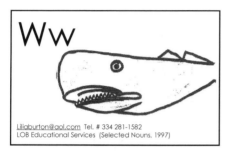

whale

A whale is a marine mammal shaped like a fish with flippers, a tail with horizontal fluke, and blowholes for breathing.

A whale travels a long distance.

wig

A wig is a human or synthetic hair worn on the head for personal adornment.

Sally wore a red wig for the Halloween party.

wri.ter   **writer**

A writer is a person who writes stories, poems, songs, novels, screenplays, and other articles.

Kim and Jen's mother is a writer for children's books.

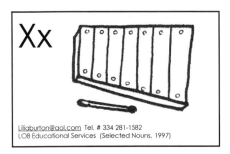

xy.lo.phone   xylophone

A xylophone is a musical instrument consisting of a series of wooden bars graduated in length to produce a musical scale.

The band played good music with xylophone.

x-ray

An x-ray is a process to .photograph, examine, or treat a part of a body.

The x-ray showed a torn ligament in my knee.

x-ray tech.ni.ci.an   technician

An x-ray technician is a person who is qualified to take x-rays to a patient.

The x-ray technician took the x-ray film to the doctor.

x-ray room

An x-ray room is a place in the hospital or a clinic where only the x-ray technician and the patient are allowed.

The x-ray technician took me to the x-ray room.

yachts.man   yachtsman

A yachtsman is a person who owns or sails a yacht. Yachtsmen takes care of their yachts.

Captain Kwisi is a yachtsman who sailed safely across the ocean.

yak

A yak is a large long-haired domesticated or wild ox.

The farmer raises yak in his farm for farming.

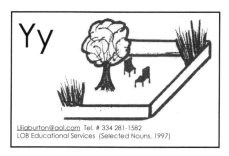

yard

A yard is a small area open to the sky and adjacent to a building. You play in a yard.

My mom and dad planted vegetables in our yard.

yo-yo

A yo-yo is a double disk with a string attached to its center. A yo-yo on a string rises and falls by unwinding and rewinding.

Solomon won first prize in a yo-yo contest.

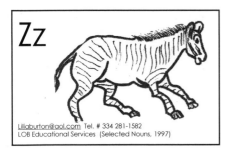

Liliaburton@aol.com Tel. # 334 281-1582
LOB Educational Services (Selected Nouns, 1997)

zeb.ra   **zebra**

A zebra is a horse-like African mammal. A Zebra has black or brown and white stripes.

The children saw a zebra during their visit at the zoo.

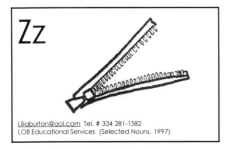

Liliaburton@aol.com Tel. # 334 281-1582
LOB Educational Services (Selected Nouns, 1997)

zip.per   **zipper**

A zipper is a fastening device with rows of metal, plastic, or nylon teeth.

My zipper broke when I forced open my pants.

Liliaburton@aol.com Tel. # 334 281-1582
LOB Educational Services (Selected Nouns, 1997)

zoo

A zoo is a place which living animals are kept and exhibited to the public.

I took my grandchildren to a zoo last week.

Liliaburton@aol.com Tel. # 334 281-1582
LOB Educational Services (Selected Nouns, 1997)

zoo.keep.er   **zookeeper**

A zookeeper is a person whose job is taking care of the animals in a zoo.

The zookeeper takes care of the animals very carefully.

References

Alabama Course of Study: *English Language Arts*. Bulletin (1999). Alabama State Department of Education. Montgomery, AL. U.S.A.

Armbruster, B. B., Lehr, F., & Orborn, J. (2001). Put reading first: The research building blocks for teaching children to read (kindergarten through grade 3). Center for the Improvement of Early Reading Achievement (CIERA). U.S. Department of Education.

Armbruster, B. B., Lehr, F., & Orborn, J. (2002). *A child becomes a reader: Kindergarten to grade 3.* (Report No. CS511603). Washington, DC: National Institute of Literacy. (ERIC Document Reproduction Service No. ED 470745). Retrieved January 10, from the ERIC database.

Blanchard, P. S. (2000). *Phonological awareness instruction to prevent reading failure.* (Report No. CS013983). Department of teacher education of Johnson Bible College. (ERIC Document Reproduction Service No. ED441228). Retrieved December 02, 2005, from the ERIC database.

Blankenship, T. (2003). *Wyoming early childhood readiness standards.* (Report No.PS031529). Wyoming Department of Education. Cheyene, WY. (ERIC Document Reproduction Service No. ED480653). Retrieved October 8, 2006, from the ERIC database.

Bodrova, E. & Leong, D. J. (2001). *Tools of the mind: A case study of implementing the Vygotskian approach in American early childhood and primary classrooms. Innodata Monographs 7.* (Report No.PS029660). International Bureau of Education, Geneva, Switzerland. (ERIC Document Reproduction Service No. ED455014). Retrieved March 08, 2006, from the ERIC database.

Brooks, M & Engmann-Hartung, D. (1976). *Pro.ed.* Pad (#1079). Shoal Creek Blvd. Austin, TX.

Carbo, M., Dunn, R., & Dunn, K. (1991). Teaching students to read through their individual learning styles. Needham Heights, MA. Prentice-Hall, Inc.

D'Arcangelo, M. (2003). On the mind of a child: A conversation with Sally Shaywitz. (Item No. 9490591). *Association For Supervision and Curriculum Development.* (ERIC Document Reproduction Service No. EJ666021). Retrieved March 04, 2006, from the ERIC database.

Dewey, J. (2005). *Democracy and education: An introduction to the philosophy of education.* New York, NY. Cosimo, Inc.

Educational Insights, Inc. (2000). Rancho Dominguez, CA.

Lambert, L., Walker, D., Zimmerman, D. P., Cooper, J. E., Lambert, M. D., et. al. (2002). *The constructivist leader* (second edition). Oxford, OH. Teachers College Press.

Leafstedt, J.M., Richards, C. R., & Gerber, M. M. (2004). Effectiveness of explicit phonological awareness instruction for at-risk English-learners. (Article No. 14603627). *Learning disabilities research and practice.* Camarillo, CA. (ERIC Document Reproduction Service No. EJ687018). Retrieved January 10, 2006, from the ERIC database.

Merriam-Webster (1994) Merriam-Webster's Elementary Dictionary. Springfield, MA. U.S.A. Marriam-Webster Inc.

Merriam-Webster (1988) Webster's Collegiate Thesaurus. Springfield, MA. U.S.A. Marriam-Webster Inc.

Merriam-Webster (1981). The New Merriam-Webster Dictionary. Springfield, MA. U.S.A. Marriam-Webster Inc.

Norman, K. A. & Calfee, R. C. (2004). Tile test: A hands-on approach for assessing phonics in the early grades. *The Reading Teacher.* International Reading Association.

Smith, C. B. (2003). *Phonological awareness*. ERIC topical bibliography and commentary. (Report No. CS512433). ERIC clearinghouse on reading, English and communication. Bloomington, IN. (ERIC Document Reproduction Service No. ED480635). Retrieved November 11, 2005, from the ERIC database.

Speece, D. L. & Ritchey, K. D. (2005). A longitudinal study of the development of oral reading fluency in young children at risk for reading failure. (ISSN Number 00222194) *Journal of Learning Disabilities, volume 38* (n5), p387-399 Sep-Oct 2005. (ERIC Document Service No. EJ722266). Retrieved September 4, 2006, from the ERIC database.

Steiner, R. (1997). *Education as a force for social change*. Hudson, NY. Anthroposophic Press.

Tyner, B. (2004). *Small-group reading instruction: A differentiated teaching model for beginning and struggling readers*. (Report No. CS512501). International Reading Association, Newark, DE. (ERIC Document Reproduction Service No. ED480254). Retrieved February 06, 2006, from the ERIC database.

Woods, C.S. (2002). Building a Stairway to Literacy with the Montessori Movable Alphabet. (ISBN No. 105400400). *Montessori Life*. (ERIC Document Reproduction Service No. EJ657979). Abstract retrieved May 06, 2006, from the ERIC database.

Work, B (2002). *Learning through the eyes of a child: A guide to best teaching practices in early education*. (Report No.PS030891). North Carolina State Department of Public Instructions, Raleigh, NC. (ERIC Document Reproduction Service No. ED472193). Retrieved March 08, 2006, from the ERIC database.

Vygotsky, L. (1986). (revised and edited by Kozulin, A.). *Thought and language*. The Massachusetts Institute of Technology, Cambridge, Massachusetts. The MIT Press.

Index